An Uncommon Bond

An Uncommon Bond

*A Story of Faith,
Forgiveness, and Friendship*

Jay R. Townsend

To my wife and children – my world.

Table of Contents

The Incident

Buddy

Buddy Johnson caught the basketball from the official and glanced up at the scoreboard. His 5'10" slender body was drenched in sweat. His team was down one point with no time left on the clock. The previous play he stole the ball and was on his way in for a game winning layup when he was hammered by the opposing teams 6'4" center as time expired. The scoreboard displayed Vikings 75, Tigers 74. If he made these two free-throws his team would win and advance to the Regional Championship game. If he missed the season would be over.

Since he was fouled with no time remaining, he was the only person at the free-throw line. He had done this millions of times. He thought back to a basketball camp he went to several years ago. He was taught to develop a routine. Catch the ball. Find the center of the free-throw line. Two dribbles. Take a deep breath. Elbow under the ball. Lift the ball up and over the rim. Follow through. Swish. Automatic. Every time. He felt confident.

Buddy went through his progression. The crowd from the visiting teams section was making loud noises to distract him. He zoned out the crowd and took the shot. Once he released it he knew the shot was off. He could tell it was going to be short and it was. Boing! Off the front of the rim. It had no chance of going in. The opposing crowd went nuts. He stepped back and gathered his composure. If he made this second shot, they could at least tie and go into overtime.

He went through his progression again. He wasn't going to leave this one short. He lifted the ball up and over and followed through. It felt good and looked good. It hit the back of the rim, bounced up and hit the backboard, came back down and hung on the rim. It felt like time stood still. Then the ball slowly rolled off the side of the rim and the game was over. The opposing team and crowd were jumping up and down and hugging. Buddy looked over at his coach and teammates. He saw the disappointment in their eyes. He felt the anger and ache in his heart of losing. How could this happen to him? He was supposed to be the hero! Not today. This was one of the worst feelings in the world.

Buddy hung his head and made his way to the locker room. He was fuming. He had never felt so embarrassed in his life. Buddy didn't realize it, but what happened to him tonight, would change his life forever.

Carl

Carl Ross sat in the very top right section of the gymnasium. He didn't get out a lot, but knew the game tonight would be a good one. It didn't disappoint. He missed sports. The sound of the whistle. The smell of popcorn in the air. The roar of the crowd. For many years now Carl liked to keep to himself. His once wavy black hair and thick beard had specks of gray in it. He was still tall and

4

muscular. He tried to jog and lift weights every morning bright and early, but old age and drinking beer were catching up to him!

He had a slight smirk on his face as he watched the basketball game unfold before him. He couldn't get over how much Buddy Johnson looked like his Father. Right around 5'10 to 6'0" tall. Lanky kid. Short crew cut blond hair. He looked like a basketball player, and as a senior he played like a basketball player. His eyes. Man did he have his Mother's bright blue eyes. It brought back a lot of memories for Carl.

The kid had played one outstanding game. According to Carl's mental math, which he always did for some reason during games, was that Buddy Johnson had 27 points, 7 rebounds, and 12 assists.

Man did he make his team better when he was on the floor. The other aspect that made him raise his eyebrows was that he didn't turn the ball over. As a senior the kid was good, if not even better than his father Kevin which was saying a lot. But at the end of the game, Carl saw Buddy falter on his last two free-throws. He missed short on his first free-throw and had the ball roll out on his last free-throw. He saw the disappointment on the face of Buddy. He felt sorry for the kid.

Carl lowered his head and eyes and shuffled out of the gymnasium with all the other fans. Back home to an empty house. Carl didn't realize it, but his life would change very soon, and it would involve a tall lanky kid named Buddy Johnson.

Buddy

Buddy took off his soaked jersey and threw it against his locker in the locker room. His locker was open and he kicked it shut as hard as he could. Bang! Coach Robertson came in and said, "settle down, settle down."

The team, some players with tears in their eyes turned their attention to coach Robertson.

"Gentlemen, I know the outcome of the game was not in our favor. But I'm proud of you. You never gave up and fought hard to the end. So, in my mind, we are all winners."

Buddy thought to himself, "except for me. I let the team down. This was my fault." His blood started to boil.

Coach started talking again. "The key is to learn from this game, work hard in the off-season, and come back next year even better. I want to thank you for all of your hard work this year. Especially all the seniors. Bring it in."

The team huddled up and for the last time this season said "Tigers on 3 – 1..2..3..TIGERS!"

Buddy took a long, hot shower to soak his aching muscles. He just wanted to be left alone. His high school basketball career was over and he was fuming about the missed free-throws. He got dressed and was about to leave the locker room when he overheard his good friend Dustin make a comment that made him stop in his tracks. Dustin was on the other side of the lockers and didn't know Buddy could hear him.

Dustin said, "all he had to do was at least make one. One free-throw and we could have won in overtime. How hard is it to make at least one out of two free-throws?"

Something in Buddy snapped.

Buddy stomped around the corner and said, "You could have done better Dustin? What did you do this game? Turn the ball over? Miss like 10 shots?"

Dustin stared at him with his mouth half open. He had never seen Buddy act this way before.

Yelling now Buddy said, "That is what I thought. You just need to shut your face and worry about yourself. I'm outta here!"

Buddy stormed out of the locker and slammed the door on his way out.

9

Buddy started walking home. Who do some of these guys think they are? Don't they know I carried the team tonight? If it wasn't for me, we would have lost by double digits! They have no respect or appreciation for me. None. Buddy started to dribble the ball he always carried with him. Between the legs, around the back, quick cross over. The ball was like an extension of his body. Buddy was deep in thought. How did he miss both free-throws? He was the best free-throw shooter on the team. Ugggg!

He was about halfway home when he looked to his left and saw the old basketball courts he used to play on in middle school. The school had shut down several years ago and weeds were sprouting up on the court. The old hoop was still up, but about half the chainlink net was missing. A dull light produced enough light to take a few shots, especially free-throws. Buddy made a deal with himself. He needed to make 30 free-throws in a row to go home. If he missed just once, he had to start over.

An hour had gone by and he had not even made it to 25 in a row. His frustration level was about to explode. He was yelling at himself "come on! Concentrate." He threw the ball against the fence as hard as he could. His blood was boiling! He picked up the ball and kicked it with all of this strength. The ball disappeared into the night sky. Then sudden fear struck his heart. He realized the ball was soaring towards a rundown white house. It wasn't just any house. Buddy and his friends had talked about this house. They knew very little about the owner. Buddy had seen him around town before.

He had a rugged look to him. A scruffy beard. He always seemed to keep his head and eyes down. What did they call him?? Crazy Carl. That was it. Not good. Not good at all! Then it happened.

The ball zipped down and shattered a window on the top level of the house. In the quiet evening, the sound of the crash was extremely loud. Buddy hesitated on what to do next. Then his adrenaline kicked in and he took off running for home as fast as he could. He sprinted through a dark alley and cut through old man Thompson's back yard. When he felt like he was in the clear he slowed down and eventually stopped. His hands were shaking, and he was drenched in sweat. Crazy Carl. Buddy was certain the old man didn't see him. The house was dark. He was in the clear. He stood up and started to make his way for home. Then all of a sudden he stopped. Not good. Buddy put both hands over his face and groaned. He realized that the ball he kicked, his ball, had his name written on it.

Carl

Carl walked up the sidewalk to his house, unlocked the door, and entered closing the door softly. He stood in the entryway and took in the dark silence. The house seemed dead. He could hear the hum of his fridge and the tick tock of a clock in the living room. He felt like the house. Empty.

He briefly thought back to the day he and his wife purchased this house. He never thought he would move to rural North Dakota. They both were born and raised in Montana. However, teaching jobs became available in Tyler, North Dakota (home of the Tigers!) and they made it home. They loved the location and the small-town atmosphere. A lot of wonderful memories were made in this community and house.

He tossed his keys on the table and flicked on the light in the kitchen. He opened the fridge and peeked inside. His choices consisted of milk or beer. He chose a beer. He twisted the top off the bottle, tossed it in the garbage and sat down in his recliner. Tonight brought back a lot of memories. A lot to process.

It had been 17 years since the incident. He relived it every day in his mind. It changed his life in an instant. Before the incident happened, he had always heard of people talking about "life changing moments" and after what happened to him, he finally understood. He knew he wasn't the only person affected by what happened. At the same time, he knew he fell the hardest after it happened.

He was deep in thought in his living room when he heard a familiar noise coming from outside. Thump. Thump......Thump. Thump. Thump......Thump. The light was off in the living room, so he walked over to the window and peeked out. He had to smile. Across the street shooting free-throws was none other than Buddy Johnson. The kid had determination. Carl watched as Buddy took two dribbles, a deep breath, released the ball with perfect form and rotation and made the shot. The kid hit about 20 in a row when he missed one short. He watched as Buddy yelled at himself and slammed the ball on the ground. He started shooting free-throws again. Swish. Swish. He was on a roll. Buddy had made again around 20 to 25 shots when he missed.

What happened next blew Carl's mind. The kid grabbed the ball and threw it as hard as he could against the fence. He then, in pure anger, kicked the ball as hard as he could. He looked like a punter in the NFL! The ball was headed right towards Carl's house. Carl looked up as it sailed towards his roof. Then he heard a loud crash from the upper level of his house.

He shifted his eyes back to the basketball court and watched as Buddy Johnson stood frozen for a few seconds on the court. Then in a flash took off in a dead sprint down an alley and out of sight.

Carl liked the fire the kid had but he needed to learn to control his emotions. He made his way upstairs to a room he had not been in for years. He opened the door and flicked on the light. He glanced to his right and saw his desk the way he had left it many, many years ago. He looked straight ahead and took in the damage. The basketball had completely shattered the window. The ball was laying in the middle of the room. He went over, put his foot on top of the ball, rolled it towards him and quickly move his foot under the ball and flicked it up into his hands. He spun the ball in his hands and then stopped it instantly. He looked down and saw scribbled on the ball the name, Buddy Johnson.

Carl turned around and walked back to the doorway. He stopped to turn off the light and took one more glance at the room. What an evening. If seeing Buddy Johnson tonight brought back a lot of memories, this room opened a flood of memories. He shook his head and flicked off the light and closed the door.

After going to the garage and putting a tarp over the window, Carl sat at the kitchen table trying to decide what to do next. His palms were sweating and he could feel the adrenaline throughout his body. He walked into the living room and sat down in his recliner again. He put his elbows on his knees and did something he had not done in 17 years. He prayed. He asked God to give him a sign of what to do. He sat in silence and then all of a sudden he about jumped out of his skin. The clock in the living room had an hourly chime and it dinged loud and clear. Carl shook his head. This is stupid. Asking God for help. For answers! He turned on the lamp and looked up at the clock on the mantle above the fireplace. That is when Carl saw it! On the mantle next to the clock was his Bible.

He walked over and took it off the mantle. He blew the dust off it and sat back down. He loved the smell of books. The cover was worn. He flipped through the pages and saw verses underlined and highlighted. Little notes he scribbled in the margins. He closed the book and glanced over at the phone. God had spoken and he knew what he needed to do. He found a phone book and looked up the number. He took a deep breath and dialed. He heard the other end of the line pick up.

"Hello" the female voice said.

Carl said, "Lily, it's uh… coach Ross. We need to talk."

Buddy

Buddy was stretched out on his bed with the lights off. The only light in his bedroom came from the laptop on his desk. The night had been a disaster. Not only did he let his team down and friends down, to top it all off he shattered a window at a house that belonged to none other than crazy Carl. When he arrived home his Mom tried to talk to him, but Buddy was not in the mood. He totally ignored her and headed straight for his bedroom. He saw the hurt in her eyes. He didn't know if that hurt was from her disappointment of him losing the game or with him giving her the cold shoulder. He loved his Mom a lot, but lately it seemed like an imaginary wall had developed between them. They had both always needed each other and he felt that bond starting to crack.

Buddy just wanted to disappear. He didn't want to see the headlines tomorrow on the game that he lost. He didn't want to see his coach and teammates lower their eyes when he saw them. He wanted it all to go away. The other thing that kept itching at the back of his mind was his Dad. How could he miss somebody so much that he does not have any memory of? He heard the comments. "You look so much like your Dad" or "you play basketball just like your Dad did back in the day." He had no memory of his Dad. Several times he asked his Mom about him, but she was vague about any answer. He can still see the hurt in her eyes over his death so Buddy stopped asking.

As Buddy was deep in thought, he heard the phone ring out by the kitchen. His Mom answered it and he could hear her muffled responses deep in conversation with somebody. Buddy figured it was either the police or crazy Carl. Boy did he get himself into a pickle. This wasn't going to be good. After several minutes, which seemed like an hour, he heard a light knock on his door.

"Come in," said Buddy.

His Mom peeked around the corner. "Hey, Bud."

"Hey, Mom."

"I just got a phone call from Coach Ross. He said he heard some noise outside his house and when he looked out he saw you kick a ball that shattered a window in an upstairs room at his house. You want to talk to me about that?"

"I'm sorry Mom." He now had the urge to cry. He hated crying. "I was just so frustrated about the game. About letting the team down. I lost my temper. Did he call the cops?"

"Who? Coach Ross? He would never do that."

"Why do you call him Coach Ross?" asked Buddy.

Lily raised her eyebrows. "Well, that is a long story for another time. But coach…I mean Carl…I mean Mr. Ross does want something."

"What's that?" said Buddy.

His mom had a half smile on her face when she said, "tomorrow he wants you at his house at 8:00 AM sharp."

Carl

Carl hung up the phone and had to smile. It felt good to talk to Lily Johnson after all these years. A flood of memories seeped back into his brain. Most memories good and one memory very, very bad.

Kevin and Lily Johnson dated since what seemed like elementary school. You would never see one without the other. Carl watched them blossom during high school as student-athletes. Kevin was the typical small-town jock. He was all-state in football, basketball, and track. Basketball was his best sport. He went on after high school and played four successful years in college. But what did Carl love best about him? His leadership and influence he had not only at school but also in the community. Lily was a track star. She was one of the best 800-meter runners he had ever seen. She just looked natural – a pure runner. Lily also went to the same college as Kevin and had four successful years in track. Lily wasn't as outgoing as Kevin was, but she was just as influential and a very hard worker. They both were just great kids.

What impressed Carl the most was what they accomplished at their weekly Fellowship of Christian Athletes group studies or "huddles" as they were called. Carl loved FCA. It brought together student-athletes and inspired them to live a life like Jesus. A life of significance. Carl was the "huddle coach" and Kevin and Lily were the "huddle leaders". The amount of influence they had on the school and community from what they did at FCA over the four years was unbelievable. It was truly amazing to see and experience.

After college Kevin and Lily where married and both landed jobs at the same high school they graduated from. Lily was the school counselor. Kevin taught physical education and health classes. Kevin also coached football, basketball, and baseball. After a couple of months on the new job Lily found out she was pregnant. The couple couldn't be more excited. It truly was the American dream. Then in a blink of an instant everything changed.

Buddy

Buddy argued with his Mom until he was blue in the face. He couldn't believe she was going to make him go to the house of crazy Carl. It sounded like he was spending the whole morning with him! Was she crazy! The guy was weird. He was always grubby. He had a scruffy beard. He always walked around town with his head down. Something wasn't right about this guy.

Buddy crawled into bed and stretched his long legs and yawned. What a night. Well, if his Mom wanted him to do this he would. It would be a waste of time, but he would do it. He could tell it meant a lot to his Mom for some reason. As he started to drift off to sleep, he thought of his Dad again. Man, how could you miss somebody so much you have never even met?

Carl

Carl crawled into bed and set his alarm for 5:30 AM. He loved his morning jog. It helped him stay in shape and at the same time it gave him time to think. He had only been doing his morning jogging routine within the last year because he usually still had a mild hangover the next morning. But now, he loved the feeling when he was done and drenched in sweat. That feeling of knowing you worked hard to accomplish something. He turned off his bedside lamp and stared up at the ceiling. He wondered how tomorrow would go? How would

Buddy Johnson handle what he had planned for him? It would be interesting that was for sure.

As with most nights, Carl's mind went back to the night that changed everything. They were having one of the best basketball seasons in school history. Kevin Johnson was the head coach and Carl was his trusty assistant coach. They had played their rival that night and had won on a buzzer beater. The excitement carried from the locker room to the bus ride home. It was winter and the roads were snow packed. Visibility was low. A true North Dakota blizzard. As they came around a bend in the road, they saw what looked like headlights in the ditch. Kevin instructed Darold the bus driver to pull over.

Kevin and Carl threw on their winter gear and told Darold to call 911. The night was cold and very windy. They approached the lights and could see a vehicle had went off the road and spun so the back end was halfway in the Wild Rice River and starting to slowly sink.

Kevin yelled, "We have to see if anyone is still in the vehicle!"

They each took a side of the vehicle and looked inside. They could see a Mom and her infant son. Both were unconscious but looked to be breathing.

Kevin yelled, "We have to get them out of here! The car is sinking!"

Carl was in shock. He finally snapped out of it. They went to work. Kevin jumped into the vehicle through the shattered back window. He unbuckled the boy and handed him to Carl. The car buckled and went farther into the water. They didn't have much time. Carl laid the boy down. He looked up and could tell time was critical. He could see Kevin working to get the Mom unbuckled and trying to get her door open.

Carl yelled, "Hurry! Hurry!"

Carl reached in and used all his strength to help Kevin pull and the mom finally slid out and landed on top of him. Carl rolled her off him and looked up. It was the last time he saw Kevin Johnson alive. Kevin almost had a peace to him as he made eye contact with Carl and then the car went under.

Carl blamed himself. It should have been him in the car. Kevin had a whole life and family ahead of him. Carl would never forgive himself.

Challenge #1

Buddy

Buddy Johnson looked up at the untidy house in front of him. He looked at his cell phone and the time showed 7:55 AM. He would rather be anywhere else in the world than where he was at right now. Especially on a Saturday.

He walked up to the door and knocked. He could hear a gruff voice say, "hold on" and then seconds later the door opened up and he came face to face with crazy Carl. Buddy first noticed that the man in front of him up close looked a lot younger than he thought. He could tell he was physically fit and had a sparkle to his eyes. He had graying hair and a shaggy beard. His clothes were worn but not horrible. He had a calmness to him. He made Buddy feel something. Almost comforted or relaxed. He couldn't help but feel a touch of regret of the way he judged him all these years.

Carl said, "Hello Buddy, my name is Carl. It is a pleasure to meet you."

Carl stuck out his hand. Buddy reluctantly took his hand. He had a firm handshake and he could feel callouses on his hands. Carl kept eye contact with Buddy the whole time. "Come on in. We have a lot to talk about," he said as he waved Buddy in over his shoulder.

Buddy followed Carl into the house. Inside it was quite clean and tidy. Off to the right was the kitchen and to the left was the living room area. He followed Carl into the living room. Carl said, "Have a seat here on the couch. You want something to drink? Soda? Water?"

Buddy said, "I'll take a soda."

"All I have is diet. Hope that's ok." He disappeared into the kitchen.

This gave Buddy some time to take in his surroundings. Not much to take in. The walls were almost completely empty. A clock was on the fireplace mantel and by the clock was a picture. He could tell it was a younger version of Carl (minus the beard) with a woman. She had blonde hair. They both had huge smiles on their faces. It looked like they were at a sporting event at a large stadium. He could see a lot of people wearing the color red. He just couldn't quite make out the team. He saw by the recliner a book. It was worn. It was a Bible. He had seen a similar looking Bible somewhere but couldn't place it. Just then, Carl came into the room carrying a couple of drinks.

He handed Buddy the soda and sat down. "We need to talk about the broken window, first, you are going to help me fix it. We will do it together."

"Ok" said Buddy. "I'm really sorry about what happened. I lost my cool."

Carl raised an eyebrow. "Lost your cool. Looked a little more than that. But we will get to that. My first rule is that when we meet you will bring a notebook and a pen. You will keep a journal. This isn't a normal journal. Don't write down what we did or anything like that. Write down what you learned. Write down any "take aways" from what we discuss. Understand?"

Buddy was looking at him with his mouth half open "I think I got it." This guy was intense. Carl stood up. "Well, that window isn't going to fix itself. Let's go!"

Carl

It felt good to have another human being in his presence. Carl missed the socialization aspect of his life. He was always a "people person" and having Buddy work beside him on the window was a breath of fresh air.

"So, how's school going?"

"Ok I guess", said Buddy.

"Grades ok?"

"Yeah, I get mostly A's and B's."

"Good to hear."

Carl was a handy man. He loved doing odd jobs and tinkering around in his garage. Over the years he had become skilled in handyman work. It excited him to teach Buddy these skills. Especially since Buddy didn't have a father figure to learn from. Carl knew all too well about that. His Dad was the town drunk. If he wasn't yelling at his Mom, he was at the bar yelling at the bartender. He never had the experience or comfort of a loving father. After high school, Carl left home and never looked back. He felt trapped. The walls in his home growing up felt like they were closing in on him. He felt bad for leaving his mom, but he needed a new start.

The first few years of college were not good either. The freedom went to his head and he did things he was not proud of. Then his life changed on two accounts his junior year in college. He met two people. One, he met Jesus. Two, he met his future wife. After two years of fun he decided to get serious and focus on his studies. He loved coaching and working with youth, so he got his degree as an educator. During that time, he met his future wife Beth at a college function. He can still remember the day after football practice overhearing a few of his teammates talking about something called FCA. When he asked them what that was, they told him Fellowship of Christian Athletes. They invited him to their meeting or what they called "huddle". Carl

38

was hesitant to go because he seldom went to church. Growing up they would go at Easter or Christmas. His two teammates were great guys, so he decided to give it a whirl.

At that first huddle his life took a different path. He felt welcome. He dipped his toe in slowly each meeting and started to read the Bible more. He also liked to go because the most gorgeous girl he had ever laid eyes on would also attend. He found out her name was Beth. He would try to coordinate it so they would sit by each other or be in the same small group discussions. He learned to love God and Jesus. He also learned to love Beth. Both relationships, one with God and one with Beth, blossomed over the next two years. As they say, the rest is history. He became a huge advocate and leader of FCA and married the love of his life. Fast forward to the present day and those two loves in his life where both gone.

As Buddy drilled in the final screw Carl couldn't help but smile. They spent most of the day working away silently except for when Carl was instructing Buddy on the repairs to replace the window. Carl already liked the kids work ethic. You didn't see that in today's youth. It was about lunch time and Carl and Buddy picked up their tools and cleaned up their work area. "Thanks for helping fix the window", said Carl.

Buddy looked at him with dirt on his face, "This was actually fun. I mean, I've never done anything like this. It didn't even feel like work!"

"Well you did a great job. I don't know about you, but my stomach is growling. You up for a couple of burgers on the grill?"

"I'm starved", said Buddy.

As with most teenagers, Buddy could eat like a horse. He was a growing boy. Not much discussion took place while they ate.

"Well, that's all for today. Again, I appreciate you helping me with the window", said Carl.

"No problem. I still feel bad about breaking it. I'm sorry again Mr. Ross."

"Please, call me Carl. The plan from here on out is that we will meet for the next three weeks on Saturday. How about we meet at 8:00 AM next

Saturday. Also, remember to bring a notebook and a pen. We good?"

"Sounds good. Have a great day and I'll see you then."

Buddy

Buddy hated to admit it, but he enjoyed his first encounter with crazy Carl. In fact, he was ready to drop the crazy part from his name. When he told his Mom about the day and when he mentioned about seeing if he could get a notebook his Mom had a small smirk on her face. He didn't know what that meant but he had a feeling his Mom understood how this whole notebook thing worked. As he started to doze off to sleep that night, he had to wonder what the next meeting would bring with Carl.

Carl

"Write this down on the top of the first page of your notebook. First write today's date. Always date your journal entry, said Carl. Now write '*I want to be a reflection of him*'."

Buddy did as he was instructed and thought to himself "a reflection of who?"

Carl looked up at the ceiling deep in thought and then said, "here is what we are going to do. We will meet for the next three weeks like I said before. I will give you three challenges over this time period. Your job will be to accomplish these challenges and then come back and discuss them with me each weekend. Does that make sense?"

"I think so", said Buddy.

"Good. Now while you complete these challenges, I want you to write in your journal. Write down what you are learning from these challenges. Write down those "a-ha" moments."

Buddy was deep in thought. "How do I tell if it is a "a-ha" moment or not?"

"You'll know" said, Carl. "It will become habit eventually. Always strive to learn from every situation. Seek knowledge. Analyze mistakes. Learn from them."

Buddy liked what Carl was telling him so he started to jot down what he was saying. Carl smiled. The kid was already getting it!

"Are you ready for challenge #1?", asked Carl.

"Ready or not, I guess," said Buddy.

"Ok. Here it is. On the top of your journal page write down the word SEE."

Buddy did as he was told.

Carl continued, "People today have what I call tunnel vision. What I mean by this is that they don't see the world as we should see the world. For example, they may work with a person for years and not really get to know them or connect with them. They know the person works with them. They know the person. But they never develop a *relationship* with that person. My challenge to you is to find a place at school that is centrally located. Can you think of such a place?"

"Yes, we have a commons area at school that is basically the middle of the school. A lot of kids just hang out in that area either studying or talking with friends" said, Buddy.

"Great. This week when you are in that area, I want you to check out the other students in your school. See what they are wearing. Who they hang out with. How they interact with others. Get the point?", said Carl.

"Sounds easy enough to me. Challenge accepted!" said Buddy.

"I have a side challenge for you also, Buddy if you are willing to accept," said Carl with a glimmer in his eye.

"What is that?" said Buddy.

Carl leaned forward so his elbows were on his knees and said, "go check out the trophy case right outside the gym doors. Find your dad in those pictures. Check him out when he was in high school and as a coach. Look for details. When you come back next week tell me what you saw about your dad in those pictures. Make sense?"

Buddy nodded.

"Well, that is all for today. You have your challenge and side challenge. Focus on the two challenges this week and we will be ready to talk next week. It was a pleasure visiting with you today, Buddy" said Carl as they headed to the front door.

Buddy

Buddy set up shop in the commons area Monday morning at 7:45 AM. He didn't usually get to school early, but Carl gave him a challenge and it was in Buddy's blood to not fail a challenge. He was competitive and always gave 100%. Plus, he was getting the hang of taking notes in his journal and liked the feeling of constantly writing down his observations and always learning. It seemed all situations, good or bad, he took something from. He learned from each experience.

He didn't want to seem like he was just hanging out and staring at kids, so he opened his laptop and pretended like he was working on something. As the morning went on several students started to enter the building. It felt weird what he was doing but at the same time he was amazed at what he didn't see all these years. One kid sat over in the corner with his head down. He seemed lost in his thoughts. His clothing was dirty and way too small for him. His hair was greasy. He seemed empty or lost. A girl walked by with her hair dyed green and earrings in her nose. Some of his sports friends where laughing over by the soda machine. They were wearing lettermen jackets. A group of what Buddy would call computer geeks walked by. They were talking about some online computer game. It was crazy to see the vast differences in all these kids. Some you could tell were poor. Some you could tell were very smart. The kid in the corner, well, he was a lot of things and Buddy felt regret for never noticing him ever while at school. The bell for his first hour class rang, and Buddy gathered up his things and headed for class. As he walked down the hall, he thought to himself this challenge will be harder in more ways than one.

Throughout the day he seemed more focused on watching his classmates interact than paying attention to his teachers. He was called on in class several times and felt silly when he couldn't answer the question. He was amazed and frustrated at the same time on what he gathered throughout the day in his journal. Several things tugged at his conscience on his way home from school. First, everybody has a story. He saw rich kids, poor kids, sad kids, angry kids, and so much more. He felt sorry for several kids. He was mad at other kids for the way they treated other kids. Second, he saw the kid that was sitting in the corner that morning get picked on a lot throughout the day. Buddy had never noticed this before and hoped that he never engaged in any of that behavior. It was like watching his self-esteem get chipped away with a pickaxe. He found out the kid was named Jacob. Watching what happened to Jacob just in one day made Buddy sad and mad at the same time. He wanted to talk to Carl about this for sure.

Tomorrow his plan was to go check out pictures of his dad. He had looked at them before but with this other challenge he didn't *see* his dad. He was nervous and excited at the same time. What would he find?

Carl

It was Friday. Carl was hoping Buddy was getting the point of his first challenge as the week was coming to an end. So many people go through life not seeing others the way they should be seen. He was excited to hear about Buddy's week.

As for Carl himself, he was having an up and down week. He had kept himself busy with several jobs here and there, but in the evenings, Carl had spent a lot of time in thought. Having Buddy enter his life had stirred up a lot of memories, both good and bad, and he had tried to block out the bad for many years. In fact, as he was sitting in his recliner at this moment, he thought back to the events following the death of Kevin Johnson.

The funeral for Kevin was one of the hardest things Carl had ever attended. The days following the funeral started the decline in Carl's life. He couldn't get over the fact that Kevin was the one that acted and jumped into the car to save two lives but unfortunately took his life. Kevin had a whole life in front of him. A beautiful wife and a child soon to be born. Carl felt guilt every day for hesitating in that situation. It should have been him. He should have died that night, not Kevin.

Carl went into a deep state of depression after that. He shut himself out from the outside world. He started drinking. He spent many nights at the local bar. He couldn't sleep. He didn't shave or shower. He lost his job at the school. He had thoughts of taking his own life. He hit rock bottom.

His marriage slowly fell apart. His wife urged him to get help. "Talk to somebody," she said more than once. He ignored her. They fell into a pattern. He would come home from the bar drunk. She would confront him about it. They would get into a fight. He would end up passing out on the couch or storm out of the house and drive around and drink more beer until the early morning hours. They stopped talking to each other. They drifted apart. After about six months, Beth finally had enough and moved out of the house and went to live with her mom out in Montana. After one year, Beth filed for a divorce.

That was 17 years ago. Since then Carl's life has been nothing to write about. He is a loner. He still drinks daily but has improved in controlling his alcohol consumption. He is depressed. His only job is doing handy work. When he looks back at his life his heart aches so much for Beth. He misses her. The last he heard she still lived out in Montana to be closer to family. She had remarried, but her husband passed away a couple years ago in a skiing accident.

He misses making a difference in the lives of youth. He loved his job at the local school. He loved coaching. He loved FCA. Man, these last 17 years went by fast. Now, sitting in his empty house all these years later he felt something was speaking to him. He had heard and felt it before, but it had been a long time. God was whispering to him. God had sent him a message. That message was a 17-year-old boy scheduled to meet with him tomorrow morning. Carl picked up his Bible and started reading.

Buddy

"I heard a brilliant prayer that pastor Andy Stanley once said he says to himself all the time. Here it is – *help me see as you see and do as you say*," said Carl.

Buddy quickly wrote down the prayer in his daily journal. Carl and Buddy were sitting at the kitchen table. The first thing Carl did when Buddy walked into his house that morning was handed him an FCA athlete's Bible. It was like the Bible Buddy saw the first time he came over to Carl's house on his mantel. At the time he thought it looked familiar. Now he remembered where he had seen it before. His mom had a similar one on her bedside table.

"Remember that prayer as we talk about your first challenge," said Carl. "So, tell me what you came up with on this challenge Buddy."

Buddy looked over his journal from the last week. He had several pages filled out. He looked up and said, "Well, a couple things, I'm frustrated and embarrassed."

Carl looked at him with a puzzled look on his face, "why is that?"

Buddy thought back to the week before. "Well, I did like you said. I sat at a central location and observed a lot of students. Wow, was I amazed at the different kind of kids in my school!"

Carl was nodding his head.

Buddy continued, "I felt bad for some kids. You can tell they have a rough life. They had clothes that were dirty and too small. A lot of those kids would get picked on. Then I thought maybe I have picked on those kids which is embarrassing. The more I watched the more frustrated I was because these kids should not have to go through that."

Carl looked at Buddy, "I see. Who is going to put a stop to this?"

Buddy shrugged, "I don't know. The teachers? Maybe the principal?"

Carl put both elbows on the table and said, "Nope. It is going to be you Buddy."

Buddy about fell off his chair, "Me!?! Why me?" Buddy couldn't figure this one out. He wasn't in charge of the school. Why should he be the one to put a stop to these kids being mean to other kids?

Carl said, "You are a leader. I see it on the basketball court. I have seen it when you have met with me. A leader can have a lot of influence. That influence can either be positive or it can be negative. We all can make a difference in the lives of others. That is why I wanted you to look at the pictures of your dad. Did you do that?"

Buddy thought back to just yesterday when he took some time to look in the trophy case after school. "I looked at them yesterday after school," said Buddy.

"Great," replied Carl, "what did you see?"

Buddy got a lump in his throat. "My dad looked so happy. In a lot of the pictures he had his arm draped over the person next to him. He always had a big smile on his face in all the pictures I looked at."

Carl smiled, "Bingo. Your dad was one of the best leaders I have ever met. He made those around him better. I see that in you Buddy. You have a special gift. The gift to develop positive relationships with those around you. The other students in that building, whether you like it or not, look up to you.

Buddy let what Carl said to him slowly sink in. He didn't feel any different.

"I still don't understand? What makes me special?"

Carl took a drink of his soda, "God created you. So, you are very special. We all have talents. Some people use their talents, and some don't. Plus, you are a great athlete. What a great platform to make a difference. Think of all the athletes young people see as role models. That's you in your school and in this town."

"That is a lot of pressure," said Buddy.

Carl nodded his head, "yes it is. I would also call it something else. *Opportunity*. Every day God places us in situations that give us an opportunity to make a difference in this world. How we respond to that opportunity defines who we are. Turn back to the very first page of your journal. What did I have you write on the top?"

Buddy flipped through the pages and scanned the top of the front page of his journal, "it says '*I want to be a reflection of him*'."

Carl said, "The person we want to reflect, Buddy, is Jesus. That is why I had you write that down. Have you ever seen those bracelets that say 'WWJD' what would Jesus do?"

Buddy nodded, "Yeah, I've seen those."

"Well, when I was growing up, I didn't really understand what that meant. Then I started going to FCA in college and I started reading the Bible. Then I understood. Jesus is the greatest man to ever walk this earth and I knew then I wanted to do everything I could to be a reflection of him. I want you to strive for that also. Ok. Now I want you to take about five minutes to come up with some reflection questions you have for me on this first challenge. Then we will take a break and order a pizza and come back together and discuss your questions."

Carl

Carl was very impressed with the morning and the discussion he was having with Buddy. He saw a lot of Kevin in him. In fact, he saw a lot of himself in Buddy. It felt good again to drink up God's word and mentor another human being. Buddy was doing an excellent job of constantly learning. He had several pages of his journal filled out. Not many people always strive to learn daily. Buddy was like a sponge so far absorbing everything they had done. It was a blessing to see.

Buddy

Buddy took a bite of pepperoni pizza and wiped his hands on a napkin, "I have a question."

"Shoot," said Carl.

Buddy took a sip of his Mountain Dew, "what image of Jesus should I try to reflect?"

Carl put his hands together and rubbed them excitedly, "this is one of my favorite topics! To give you an idea on how to reflect Jesus let me tell you a condensed version of my life. I had somewhat of a messed-up childhood. We were poor. We lived in what I would basically call a shack. My mom was a very hard worker but with the stress from work and my father, she wasn't the most loving person. My dad was an alcoholic. He beat me and my mom. I would call him abusive. I was a good kid for the most part. Did ok in school. I was an athlete like you. If it wasn't for sports I think I would have gone down the wrong road. My high school basketball coach was like a father to me. He was a great man. Once I graduated from high school I left home and never looked back. I won't even go into some of the stuff I did the first couple of years in college. It was my junior year of college when everything changed."

Carl stopped and took a bite of pizza. Buddy loved stories like this, and Carl was a great storyteller.

Carl swallowed his pizza and started up again, "I was invited to a meeting called Fellowship of Christian Athletes. I was hesitant to go but my buddy kept bugging me about going, so I finally caved. The discussion at the meeting that night was about what we are talking about right now – how can we be more like Jesus? After that night my life slowly changed."

Buddy was now taking notes, "how exactly did you change? Was it some mythical power that entered your body? Did Jesus talk to you?"

Carl smiled, "no it wasn't that. I studied the Bible a lot and went to more FCA meetings. After that not only did I change as a person but *my way of life* changed also. You see Buddy, to be a follower of Jesus, I think we need to focus on one Bible verse. That verse is John 13:34 and it says 'a new command I give you: Love one another. As I have loved you, so you must love one another'. Look it up in your Bible."

Buddy looked down at his Bible. He didn't know how to look something up in a Bible. Carl was very patient and took his time explaining to Buddy the proper way to use a Bible. Buddy found the verse and underlined it with a pencil.

Buddy was in deep thought and said, "So how did this verse change your life?"

Carl said, "To be like Jesus you have to love one another. Now I know that the word 'love' is a strong word and can mean different things. As individuals we need to recognize that we are all made in the image of God and that both God and Jesus love us. I started loving other people like Jesus loves us and my life changed. Here are some examples I will give you. I treated people with respect. I volunteered at a homeless shelter. I started

67

listening to Christian contemporary music. I read the Bible daily. I held the door for people. I prayed. I took every opportunity I could to love those around me. Instead of making fun of people I loved and served them. Instead of using foul language I used words of inspiration. I started hanging out with different people. I thought of others first. Did my life change? It changed dramatically. I'm excited to see how it can change your life also."

Buddy felt like his brain was going to explode. The morning session had a lot of information packed into it and went by fast. Carl had excused himself to use the restroom. Before he left, he told Buddy to finish up any writing he had in his journal and that when he returned, they would review challenge #1 and then he would give him challenge #2 for the up and coming week. Buddy

was excited and overwhelmed at the same time.

Challenge #2

Carl

Carl grabbed a couple more drinks from the fridge and sat back down at the table. "I think we have had a very productive morning. So how about we reflect on challenge #1? What are some key points you wrote down in your journal?"

Buddy flipped through his journal and said, "I like to put a star by some of the stuff I write down if I think it is really good stuff. Here is one here. You talked about having tunnel vision. I documented this big time during the week at school. I wrote down – 'all students in our school should be appreciated'. After meeting with you today, I now realize I can be that person that can make a difference and give other students a sense of being appreciated."

Carl nodded, "It basically is a simple act of kindness. In fact, it isn't that hard to do but a lot of people don't do it. Look at it this way Buddy, it is a choice. A choice to have a positive influence daily or a negative influence daily. The choice we make rubs off on those around us. What else did you write down or put a star by?"

Buddy turned to the next page, "I wrote down 'every person has a story'. It seems like every student I observed had a story to tell."

Carl took his plate over to the sink and then said, "you are correct also on that observation Buddy. That is why developing relationships with those around you is so important. I urge you to be that person. To have that positive connection with people. It is amazing what you can do if you make those around you feel appreciated because you don't know the full story of those around you. Remember, the word I wanted you to focus on was SEE for this challenge. I hope now you see people differently when you look at them."

Carl sat back down and took a drink. "How about we go over challenge #2. You ready!?"

Buddy flipped the pages of his journal to a blank page and said, "I'm ready!"

"Write the word CONNECT on the top of your page." Buddy did as he was told. "Good. This week I want you to focus on *connecting* with those around you. Developing those positive relationships daily."

Buddy was jotting down notes. He scrunched his nose and said, "can you give me an example from the Bible? I've been reading the Bible most nights now and I love to see the connection between the Bible and how I live daily."

Carl couldn't believe his ears. It had been a long time since he had seen an individual flip his life so fast towards the greatest man to ever walk on this earth. A man named Jesus.

Carl said, "I love the way you think Buddy. Tonight, look up Matthew 4:18 and you will see one of the first connections Jesus makes. You will find a verse in that reading that I hope will connect you to the point of this challenge. We can discuss that verse and how your week went this up and coming weekend. I think that is all for today. Sound good?"

Buddy stretched his arms over his head and nodded. Buddy gathered up his belongings and headed towards the door. Carl followed and said, "I really enjoyed our discussion today. I appreciate the effort you are putting into my challenges. Have a great week Buddy and I look forward to next weekend."

Buddy

It was Sunday night and Buddy was in his room laying on his bed staring up at the ceiling. He had his basketball with him. He was shooting the ball up into the air practicing on his follow through. He was seeing how close he could get it to the ceiling without hitting the ceiling. He did this for two reasons. One, to work on his shooting form. Two, because he was nervous.

Buddy had always been a shy kid. He didn't like attention. He got that from his mother. So, the challenge for this week had his head spinning. He wasn't the most outgoing individual in the world. He liked to keep to himself and hated it when attention was pointed at him. Now, Carl wanted him to be the exact opposite. This was totally out of his comfort zone.

He tossed the ball over on a pile of clothes and glanced over at his bedside table. He picked up his Bible. It was starting to show use. It wasn't like Carl's Bible, which looked like it had been destroyed by a semi-truck, but it had verses underlined and highlighted. He decided to look up the verse Carl gave him when they last met. He flipped to Matthew 4:18 and read verses 18-22. Carl said to find a verse that would connect him to this challenge. He read the verses several times. He liked verse 19 which said, "and he said to them, "follow me, and I will make you fish for people." This had to be what Carl was talking about. Jesus calling his first disciples and making that connection. Carl wanted him to do the same in his daily life. Now, he just needed to figure out and have the courage to do just that. He clicked off his lamp and burrowed under the covers for the night. As he drifted off, he felt he could accomplish this challenge also, but it was going to take some work.

Carl

It was Friday morning and Carl was shaking and sweating at the same time. It had been a long week. He decided at the beginning of the week to quit drinking cold turkey. He knew it would be a challenge and it was.

He looked at himself in the mirror and the man looking back looked weary. The shakes were finally beginning to get shorter. That was a plus. On the other hand, it was frustrating because he knew his body was getting better, but at the same time he felt awful. He thought back to Monday. He could admit after Monday that he had a drinking problem because his body felt like it had been hit by a semi-truck. His head pounded and pounded. The worst headaches he ever had happened daily. It was some of the worst pain he ever experienced. On a positive note, he was starting to pick up more odd jobs around town. Towards the end of the week his head seemed clearer, he was more outgoing, and his energy level had increased.

As he finished brushing his teeth, he wondered how the week was going for Buddy. He was excited for the weekend. He loved his, what would you call it…sessions, with Buddy. He spit out his toothpaste and rinsed his mouth. Well, one more day of work and he would get to hear all about Buddy Johnson's week.

Buddy

Rollercoaster. That is the word, if Buddy had to pick one, to sum up his week. It was Friday evening and Buddy was taking a jog around the walking path that was on the outskirts of town. He enjoyed his evening jogs because it gave him time to think. As he took the path that curved around some trees and then headed up a slight incline, he thought back to the beginning of the week.

Monday was a disaster. His goal was to make as many connections as possible and not make a fool of himself. The day started out well. He made every effort to connect with students in the hallway. He got a few weird looks but overall, he felt he was successful. Then everything went downhill when he entered the commons area. He looked over and spotted the kid Jacob that he observed get picked on most of the day during his first challenge. Was God telling him to make this connection? He felt a tug on his heart, as if something was telling him this was why he was here right now. So, he took a deep breath and approached Jacob.

"Hey, what's up?", said Buddy.

Jacob was sitting on the floor with his back up against the wall. Jacob had his head down. He didn't look up. Buddy looked around. He didn't know what to do. "Ummm, did you hear me? I said what's up?"

Nothing. Ok thought Buddy. "I'm Buddy. I just came over to say hi."

Jacob finally spoke. "Leave me alone", said Jacob half shouting. Jacob jumped up real fast and then took off down the hallway and out of sight. Buddy had never seen anybody move that quickly in his life. Jacob 1, Buddy 0.

Buddy tried to connect with Jacob during the school day. He was unsuccessful every time. He tried in the hallway, at lunch, and during class. Jacob ignored him each time. Buddy didn't get it. The final bell of the day rang, and he gathered his things up from his desk and headed towards his locker. He forgot his basketball in his gym locker so decided he better go grab that before he took off for home. He went down into the locker room, unlocked his locker, and grabbed his ball. He closed his locker and about had a heart attack when Jacob was standing about five feet from him. He was bigger than Buddy realized. He had a weird look on his face.

Buddy said, "Hi, Jacob."

Jacob sized Buddy up and down. Buddy held his gaze. Then Jacob finally spoke, "you have two options. You can continue to try and talk to me and I can punch you in the face or you can go back to your wonderful jock life, stop bugging me, and not get beat up. Bottom line is you need to leave me alone."

Buddy was scared. He had never been in a situation like this before. Something inside of him gave him a calm feeling. Buddy replied, "What did I do to you? What do you mean my wonderful jock life?"

Jacob shook his head "you've never said one word to me all school year. Now you come waltzing into school today acting like the nicest guy in the world. My world doesn't work that way. You know what you are. You are fake."

Buddy didn't like being called something he wasn't. A flicker of anger coursed through his veins. However, that feeling of calmness took over. Buddy responded, "I'm not fake."

"Whatever. But I'm warning you. Leave me alone." Jacob turned and started to leave the locker room. Something caught Buddy's eye as Jacob was walking away. An old school Chicago Bulls logo on his back pack. Buddy smiled. A plan started to develop in his mind. Jacob liked sports. Now that was a subject Buddy could talk about all the time.

As the week progressed, Buddy didn't see Jacob around. He wasn't in school on Tuesday, Wednesday, or Thursday and Buddy was getting worried. Was it his fault that Jacob wasn't showing up? Did he push too hard? He made a plan that if Jacob wasn't in school today that he would go talk to the principal about his concerns.

Buddy got to school and quickly walked down to the commons area. He came around the corner to check the spot Jacob usually sat and was relieved to see Jacob in his usual spot. He had his head down and looked even more tired and grubby. Buddy gritted his teeth and approached him. "Morning Jacob. Haven't seen you around since Monday."

Jacob looked up. "I warned you jock. Leave me alone."

Buddy sat down next to him. Jacob slightly flinched like this was foreign to him. Buddy rummaged through his backpack until he found what he was looking for. He grabbed it and thought back to the conversation he had with his mom.

"Mom, I just want to show this to him. I think it will really connect us. Please?" Buddy was holding his dad's 1986 Michael Jordan rookie card.

"I guess. But be very careful with it. Your dad loved that card. It means a lot to me."

"I will. I promise", said Buddy.

"I want to show you something that was my Dad's. He died before I was born so I never met him. On Monday I noticed on your backpack an old school Chicago Bulls logo. So, I thought you might think this is cool", said Buddy.

Jacob rolled his eyes. Buddy pulled the card out of his backpack and held it up for Jacob to look at. Jacob slowly looked over and glanced at the card. Jacob did a double take and Buddy saw a totally different person evolve. Jacob's mouth dropped and he looked at Buddy and said "A Michael Jordan rookie card! Are you kidding me!"

Buddy grinned and said, "The best to ever play the game."

Jacob nodded, "He is my favorite player of all time. I love him."

Buddy held out the card for him to take and look at. Jacob hesitated. "Go on. Have a look", said Buddy.

Jacob took it and held it like it was the most precious thing he had ever held in his life. "I love watching videos on YouTube of MJ. The guy was a legend", said Jacob.

Buddy nodded, "The guy was unreal. I started watching videos also because I feel like it gives me a connection with my dad. He has a ton of MJ stuff. So, I fell in love with MJ also."

At that moment the bell rang for first hour class. Jacob jumped up like a cat, like he did on Monday and held out his hand to help Buddy up. Buddy took it and Jacob pulled him up. The kid had a grip and was strong. Jacob handed back the MJ rookie card and started walking away. As he was rounding the corner Buddy could see a smirk on his face as he said, "I'll see you around, jock."

The end of the school day rolled around, and Buddy decided to take a gamble. He spotted Jacob at his locker and made his way over to him. Here goes nothing. "Hey, my dad had an awesome collection of early 90's Chicago Bulls stuff. My mom keeps it displayed in his office at the house. You want to come over Saturday for lunch and check it out?"

Jacob stared at him for a long moment rubbing the back of his neck. "Ummm. Saturday. Lunch. Ummm. Yeah that sounds good."

"Awesome! You know that white house down by city park? That is where I live", said Buddy.

"Yeah I know that house. I'll see you Saturday at noon. Later, Buddy."

Buddy headed for the exit door and couldn't wait to tell Carl about his week. He also was excited about one other thing. Jacob called him Buddy, not jock!

Challenge #3

Carl

Carl took a sip of his coffee, set down his cup, and reached his arms over his head and stretched out his back. He loved the smell of the early morning and sitting out on his back porch listening to the birds chirp and sipping on a nice strong cup of coffee. He was excited to hear about how the week went for Buddy. He heard the doorbell and yelled through the screen door for his guest to come in.

He heard the door open and close and moments later Buddy came out with a cup of coffee himself. "Didn't know you were a coffee drinker", said Carl.

"It's my mom's fault. She got me hooked a couple of years ago. How are you doing old timer?"

For some reason Carl liked that Buddy had started calling him "old timer". I guess a nickname can make a person feel like they have entered that new stage of friendship. Carl said, "I'm surviving. It was good week. Work picked up so that was good. More importantly how was your week? You ready to go over this challenge #2?"

Buddy took out his journal, "Oh, I'm ready. You are going to be impressed!"

"As I remember, the word or focus of the week was CONNECT. So, tell me first about the Bible verses I wanted you to read. Matthew 4:18-22. What jumped out at you?"

Buddy checked his notes and flipped open his Bible to a page he had bookmarked. "I really liked verse 19 where it says, "and he said to them, follow me, and I will make you fish for people. That verse set the tone for me this week and I would say was the foundation each day when I strived to connect with people."

Carl nodded. "Explain."

"Well, when I focused and meditated on that verse it seemed to tell me that Jesus is the key. So, if I follow him, and people follow or *connect* with me, then essentially, they are following Jesus. I can be that light in the lives of others."

"Excellent way of explaining that Buddy. I couldn't have said it better myself. So, talk to me about any connections you may have made this week."

"It was amazing. Do you remember the kid I told you about that was always getting picked on? His name is Jacob."

"I remember. Go on."

"Well, Monday I approached him and tried to connect with him. He threatened to punch me in the face if I didn't leave him alone! Then he was gone Tuesday, Wednesday, and Thursday and I started to worry. But then he was back in school on Friday. I had a plan this time. You see, on Monday I noticed he had a Chicago Bulls backpack so on Friday I had my dad's Michael Jordan rookie card to show him. Man did he open up to me then!"

Carl smiled, "your dad did love the Bulls. I'm more of a Larry Bird fan but keep going."

"Then on Friday I asked him to come over for lunch today and he said yes. I'm really excited because he seems so sad or I would even use the word hollow if that makes sense."

Carl replied, "it makes sense. Developing lasting relationships and trust takes time. Go slow with this. From what you are telling me this Jacob needs a friend. Just remember what we discussed about *seeing* people and being that light for them."

Buddy sat back in his chair and pondered the next question he had for Carl.

"I know Jacob is only one small example of people hurting in this world. How do we reach all the others when we have so many?"

Carl answered, "Think about the Bible verse we just talked about. As Christians we need to reflect Jesus. We may not be able to reach everybody in this world, but we need to "fish for people" and lead them to Jesus also. We can do this no matter where we are and try to live a life of significance. I see that in you Buddy. You can make a difference. We all can."

Buddy was taking notes in his journal. Soaking it all in. Carl loved that about him. His desire for continuous improvement.

Carl asked his next question, "how did you feel about this week. I could tell you were a bit nervous going into this second challenge."

Buddy was nodding, "It was hard at first. I'm not the most out-going kid in the school. I hate it when attention is on me. However, as the week went on, and I interacted with more people, I felt better about myself. It made me feel good to greet people with a smile and get a smile in return."

"I agree", said Carl. "Connecting with people was a strength of mine. I must admit lately it has not been. I miss it. I understand what you are saying when it feels good to make others smile. I'm glad this last week was a great learning experience for you."

"It sure was", said Buddy.

Carl took a long sigh "well, we are down to our last challenge. Challenge #3! Turn your journal to the next blank page and on the top write the word LEAD."

Buddy did as he was told.

"Great. So now this will complete what I call the servant leadership cycle. We have SEE, CONNECT, and now LEAD. As a servant leader these three words or concepts are the foundation for success. We will go over this in more detail when you come back next weekend. For today, how about we concentrate on lead?"

"Ok, I'm ready", said Buddy.

"What are some words you think of when you think of the word lead or leader?"

Buddy thought about this for a few seconds and then said, "I think of the word boss or manager."

"How about a person. Can you think of any people that are leaders?", said Carl.

"For a person I think about someone in charge. A president or maybe a coach."

Carl nodded. "Good. This week your challenge is to study and observe what it means to be a leader. A few ways to accomplish this task is to study or read about leadership. A second way is to observe individuals in a leadership role."

Buddy looked confused. "I'm not sure I understand."

Carl scratched his chin. "You have done a wonderful job writing in your journal. Do the same for this challenge. Be observant! Find and read books on leadership. Observe those around you that are considered leaders. A coach, principal, teacher. When you read your Bible, I want you to focus on

John 13:1-20. Find the answer to what it means to be a successful servant leader."

"Got it. Well, I better get going because I have Jacob coming over to the house soon. Thanks, Carl, for our session. I'll see you next Saturday, old timer!"

Carl watched as Buddy went back into the house, washed his coffee cup out, and put it in the sink. He waved to Carl and then was out the door. Saturdays had become Carl's favorite day of the week. He enjoyed talking with Buddy. He walked over to the coffee pot and poured himself a fresh cup of coffee. He felt a bit of sadness enter his body. Buddy was a senior and school was almost finished for the year. Buddy would be going off to college soon. He really connected with the kid. He was going to miss him.

He thought about next Saturday and felt butterflies in his stomach. He was going to approach Buddy with something he had been considering the past week. He sure hoped Buddy would say yes to what he had in mind.

Buddy

Buddy reflected on how the day went, and it could not have gone better. Jacob had just left his house. The day was filled with surprises. Just as planned, Jacob showed up for lunch. He was very talkative over lunch with Buddy and his mom. Buddy found out they had more in common than he realized. Jacob told them how his mom passed away from cancer three years ago. After that occurred, things went downhill for him and his dad. Because his dad missed so much work during cancer treatments, he lost his job and they lost their house. It had been a long process to put their lives back in order. With all of this going on it had put a lot of stress on Jacob and he was very grateful for the invite for lunch.

After lunch, they had a blast just hanging out. Video games, watching old Michael Jordan videos, and shooting hoops in the backyard. They talked about sports, losing a parent, and the stress of school. As the day came to an end, Buddy realized he could see himself hanging out with Jacob in the future. Buddy was grateful for having the courage to connect with Jacob.

Buddy took out his laptop and hit the power button. He had a plan for challenge #3. He would focus on two areas for this challenge. One, he wanted to look up famous successful coaches and select one to research. Two, he wanted to observe how Coach Robertson interacted daily as a leader not only on the court, but also at school as the physical education teacher.

He opened his web browser on the laptop and typed in "successful basketball coaches" into the search engine. The names Dean Smith, Mike Krzyzweski, John Wooden, and several others popped up on the screen. He started clicking links and reading and writing in his journal about each coach. Just like during his "SEE" challenge, he could tell that each coach had a unique style of leadership. Some coaches were hard nosed and confrontational. He read a lot about this on Bobby Knight. He wanted to focus more on servant leadership. After about an hour of research he decided to concentrate on the leadership style of John Wooden. The man fascinated him. Ten national championships with seven of them in a row! During this period, his teams won 88 consecutive games in a row. He rubbed his eyes and glanced at the clock. He had been doing research for almost two hours. He shut down his laptop and decided to get some shut eye. Tomorrow he would check out a book at the library on John Wooden and observe how Coach Robertson was as a leader.

Buddy left the library with his book on coach Wooden and took up his normal spot in the commons area. He was eager to dive into his book on coach Wooden. But first he knew coach

Robertson roamed the halls in the morning as hall monitor so this would be the perfect time to see how he interacted with students in a leadership role.

Seconds later, he could see coach Robertson down at the end of the hallway talking with some 9th grade boys. He must have been telling a joke because he had them laughing. Buddy took out his journal and started taking notes. First, coach Robertson must be taking lessons from Carl because he was hitting on all the points Carl and Buddy talked about. He didn't miss a single student in the hallway. He didn't have tunnel vision. In addition, each person he saw he connected with in a positive way. Coach Robertson always had a smile on his face, and you could tell he was having a positive impact on the lives of those around him. Buddy was starting to understand what it meant to be a servant leader.

The week had been busy and as it ended, he felt he had accomplished this challenge but had a lot of questions for Carl. He was ready for another Saturday session with the old timer.

Carl

Carl was just finishing his final touches on the elaborate breakfast he created for the morning session with Buddy when he heard the knock on the door and seconds later Buddy came into the kitchen. He smiled at the thought that his relationship with Buddy had evolved to the point that Buddy knocked and came right into his house.

"Morning, champ", said Carl.

"Morning, old timer", said Buddy. "It smells wonderful in here."

"I made a nice big breakfast this morning for our final session. Eggs, bacon, pancakes, toast, you name it!"

Buddy loved breakfast. It was his favorite meal of the day. "I'm starving!"

Both Carl and Buddy sat back in their chairs and pushed their plates towards the middle of the table. They were stuffed. Carl grabbed a toothpick and took a sip of coffee. "Well this is it. The final session. I'm excited to hear all about challenge #3."

Buddy rummaged through his belongings and pulled out his journal. "This was a great challenge. I do have a lot to go over and I have questions."

"How about we talk about your research on servant leadership. I asked you to read up on servant leadership and to observe an individual that you think is a servant leader in your daily life. So, can you expand on how this went for you?" said Carl.

"I think this was my favorite challenge. I learned so much. The first thing I did was a search on the internet on successful coaches. This obviously generated a huge amount of coaches. I read a lot about several coaches and came to the conclusion that I wanted to focus on John Wooden."

Carl smiled. "Coach Wooden is my favorite coach of all time. I'm glad you selected him."

Buddy continued. "I agree. The more I read about him, the more I realized that this is an individual that had a lot of positive influence on many athletes."

"So what were some leadership points you took from Mr. Wooden?"

"Well, for starters, he had a way to get his players to buy into his system without using fear. He was a calm and very organized man, but at the same time his players loved him and would do anything for him. He was very demanding and had high expectations for his athletes. What I thought was the best point I took from Mr. Wooden was that his players knew he cared about them. He loved them and would do anything for them. In return, they would do the same for him. The environment was always positive."

Carl replied, "I love the examples you gave. It's amazing what can be accomplished when a team doesn't care who gets the credit. Coach Wooden was able to create that environment. The result from his leadership was all the success his teams had each basketball season. How about observing a leadership role. Who did you observe?"

"I selected my high school coach Mr. Robertson. When I was playing for him I didn't realize how much of a positive influence he has had on me. I also had a chance to observe him interact with students at school."

"What did you see?"

"Coach Robertson is one of the most positive people I've ever met. When we talked about making connections with people, I observed that with Mr. Robertson. He makes those around him smile. He is a great influential leader. I see similarities between him and John Wooden. As servant leaders, it's never about them. It is all about others."

Carl smiled. "Did you know that Mr. Robertson played for your dad?"

Buddy couldn't believe it. "Really? I didn't know that."

"He did. Your dad's influence molded him into the leader he is today. I hope you can see, by looking at Mr. Robertson, how one person like your dad can make a difference in the world."

Buddy couldn't help but smile.

"Now one of my favorite topics to talk about. How about we dive into John 13:1-20. Discuss your thoughts on this," said Carl.

"This was what I had questions about. I don't understand how somebody as great as Jesus washed his disciples' feet. He is the teacher. They are the students. Shouldn't they be washing his feet?"

"You have already answered this question but didn't realize it. I use this example from the Bible when I think of servant leadership. What Jesus does is a game changer. This also reflects what you observed with Mr. Wooden and Mr. Robertson. Jesus sets the example of putting others first. The example of loving those around you. Jesus is the teacher and he washes the feet of his students. Since he is doing that, he is setting the example that we all should do that. Does this make sense?"

Buddy was in deep thought. "I'm still a little confused."

Carl said, "how about we look at it this way. Michael Jordan is one of the most famous sports stars ever. If people see him loving others, caring about others, modeling love towards others, what will people do?"

"They would do the same. Ok. I get it now!"

"Exactly. As a servant leader you set the standard for those around you. You are the example. As followers of Jesus our example is what people see. They see the positive influence we are making in this world. It is about living a life of significance."

Buddy was writing in his journal and then looked up, "I have a lot of notes on servant leadership. I'm eager to be that example. This has been great."

"I'm so glad you kicked that ball into my window", Carl said with a smirk. "Now, how about we do a final review of what I call the Servant Leadership Cycle. We have SEE, we have CONNECT, and we have LEAD. If you do these three acts, you will live a life of significance Buddy."

"I love this concept. I guess I have to say even though it wasn't my finest moment, I'm glad I kicked the ball into your window also!"

Carl laughed but then all of a sudden became nervous. Buddy had never seen him act this way. "I have a question for you Buddy. Something I've been considering and I think I have the courage now to do it. Will you help me with something?"

"Of course. What is it?"

"You call me old timer for a reason. I need help with something dealing with technology. Can you look somebody up for me on social media?"

Buddy pulled out his phone. "That is easy. Who are you wanting to look up?"

Carl turned a bit red. "Well, I was thinking about my ex-wife, Beth."

Buddy smiled. His fingers were going fast on his little phone. After what seemed like seconds, he handed the phone over to Carl. Carl looked down and all of a sudden a lump formed in his throat. On the screen was Beth. She had hardly changed. She was so beautiful. It was a picture of her by a lake with a mountain in the background. Beth was always seeking adventure. It looked like her thirst for the outdoors was still high on her list. He missed Beth so much.

He looked up at Buddy holding back tears and said, "Buddy, you can say no to me but I want to ask you a favor with permission from your mom."

"What's that?"

"I would like you to accompany me out to Montana to visit Beth. I need to make this right. I lost her once. I want to win her back. I'm too old to drive all that way alone. I could use the company.

You are done with school next week and we can leave soon after school is out. I would like to come over today to see if your Mom will let you go with me. Buddy, will you help me?"

Buddy didn't hesitate. "It would be my honor. I've learned so much from you. It is the least I could do. How about we go talk to my mom right now?"

With tears in his eyes Carl said, "Thanks Buddy. Thank you so much."

The Trip

Buddy

The last month had been a whirlwind for Buddy. He shattered a window, met Carl, and graduated from high school. When Buddy and Carl approached his mom about the trip out to Montana she said, yes, immediately. Buddy could tell, just like him, she had a lot of respect for Carl. The day after graduation, Buddy went over to Carl's house to map out their trip to Western Montana. From what Buddy found on social media, Beth lived up in the mountains by a little town called Cardwell. He pulled up in front of his house and saw a man wearing a large hat mowing Carl's lawn. Carl must have hired somebody to do his lawn care before they left. Buddy went up to the front door, knocked, and went in. The house was empty. Strange. He heard the lawn mower turn off outside. Buddy decided to ask the worker if he had seen Carl. He went back outside and called for the man to come over.

"Sir, have you seen Carl?" said Buddy.

The guy mowing the lawn took off his hat. Buddy did a double take. Staring back at him with a grin on his face was Carl! He was clean shaven and his hair was cut short. He looked like he was in the military. He looked so much different and a lot younger.

"You look like you can't believe your eyes, champ," said Carl with a smirk.

"I just hope I don't have to stop calling you, old timer," said Buddy with a smile.

"How about we go inside, have some lemonade, and map this trip out?"

"Sounds good to me, old timer."

They figured it would be a two to three day trip out to where Beth lived. The plan was to leave the next morning bright and early. Buddy could tell Carl was anxious and nervous at the same time.

"I'll see you tomorrow morning 6:00 AM sharp," said Carl.

Carl

Buddy drove the first portion of the trip. They figured the North Dakota roads would be easier for Buddy to navigate. Carl could navigate the Montana roads in his sleep. If Carl had planned on a nap during the trip it wasn't happening. Buddy was one talkative kid. He kept firing questions at Carl consistently and Carl loved it.

"So what is your plan when we get there?" asked Buddy.

"Don't have a plan. I do know I'm nervous as a cat," replied Carl

Carl glanced outside his window. They were going through what is called The Badlands. Beautiful country. They had just gone by the exit to Medora. Carl loved Medora. He and Beth attended the Medora Musical every year. He missed her.

"Can you tell me more about my dad? My mom is still sensitive on talking about him."

"Sure. When I think about your dad, I think of the word influence. Some people just have that ability to make others around them feel relaxed. I'm sure you have been around people like that. I've never met a person more positive than your dad. He always had a smile on his face. It would just transform the atmosphere around him. People gravitated towards him. He was a true servant leader."

Buddy teared up. "I wish I could have met him."

Carl nodded but didn't say anything. Sometimes you just didn't have an answer.

After a moment of silence Buddy asked "you talk a lot about influence. How does a person have influence daily?"

Carl thought about this for a few moments and then said "for me Buddy it is all about the word opportunity. Always remember that word in the back of your mind. On a daily basis you are going to interact with somebody. Each time you do think of it as an opportunity to influence that person in a positive way. I always think about the school principal when I taught at the school, Mr. Herbolich. He said daily he would have people in and out of his office. Some were staff members, but most were kids that were sent to the office for a behavior issue. He said when individuals came through his door he thought of the word opportunity. He could get furious at the student. He could yell at them. He could belittle them. Instead, he took each student as an opportunity to see them, to connect with them, and eventually lead them."

"Didn't he get tired of work?"

"That is what I love about Mr. Herbolich. He had to make a choice. He could go to work with the mindset that he hated his job, was tired of students, and be miserable all day. Instead, he had the mindset of being a servant leader. He thought of those students, parents, and staff members as opportunities to live a significant life. He was patient with them. He listened to them. He did all he could to help them and make them better people by taking those opportunities to just do that. I challenge you to do the same. Stay positive and make a difference in this world daily."

Buddy nodded. "I understand what you are saying. I love that concept. Thanks for sharing."

After stopping and getting fuel and snacks, they were back on the road. They were just about to enter into Montana. Carl remembered this stretch of interstate. The country was beautiful, but it wasn't until you went through Billings you started seeing mountains in the distance. He loved the mountains. The smell of the pine. The sound of a river. He missed it. He understood why Beth moved back out here. She loved the mountains as well.

Buddy and Carl talked so much, listened to music, and slept so that the trip went fast. They had spent the night in Billings and now had rolled into Whitehall around noon. They checked into the hotel and decided to get lunch. Carl loved small town food. They found a local restaurant and ordered some burgers, fries, and a drink.

"So what is the plan," asked Buddy.

"I'm not sure. I'm nervous. I think I will find her place tomorrow in the morning sometime. I'm a bit tired from the trip and think it would be good to collect my thoughts and get some good sleep."

"What are you so nervous about?" asked Buddy

Carl sat back in his chair. "I messed up our marriage because of my drinking. I lost sight of what is the most important person in my life. Remember that time is precious Buddy. Promise me when you get into a relationship and have a family that you make them a priority. I see that a lot in the world today. Kids growing up without a male influence, either because they left the home or just are not around. Can you do that for me?"

"Yes, sir"

"I also have something else on my mind that I want you to know. When you kicked that ball into my window it changed my life. You changed my life. I was in a bad spot and because of you I'm now sober and trying to put my life back together. I want to thank you, Buddy, for these past weeks. I really feel that God put you in my life for a reason."

Buddy put his head down a bit embarrassed. "You're welcome," he said with a bit of emotion in his voice.

Buddy

Buddy was in bed watching TV and peeked over and heard Carl's deep breathing. He had fallen asleep in minutes and it was only a touch after 8:30 PM. Buddy thought back to the past few weeks. He had learned so much from Carl. His life had changed also when he kicked that ball into his window. He was excited to see how the next chapter of his life would develop. He had started getting calls from coaches and a few scholarships had been offered. It was thrilling but also overwhelming. His eyes started getting heavy also and before he knew it, he was fast asleep just like Carl.

Carl

Buddy was still sleeping and Carl had already showered, shaved, and was putting on cologne. He felt like he was going on his very first date! Buddy finally started moving around and eventually woke up.

Buddy stretched and said with a grin, "it smells like you are ready for your date!"

Carl said, "Too much?"

"No, I'm just teasing you. So, do you finally have a game plan?"

"Not really. I finally came to the conclusion that I'm just going to speak from my heart."

"I like that idea."

"Well, how do I look?"

"I think you are ready. You look great."

"Wish me luck. I'm off!"

"Good luck, old timer!"

Carl took the old highway between Whitehall and Cardwell. He looked down at the piece of paper Buddy had given him with Beth's address on it and a map Buddy sketched. Somehow Buddy found all this info using his cell phone. "Technology today," thought Carl. It only took a few minutes to get to Cardwell. If the map was accurate, after going through Cardwell he would start going up the mountain. Then, a collection of cabins will appear, almost like a small little town. Beth's house number was 23. Carl could see in the distance the little "town" of cabins. It was a neat little area with several cabins spread out. It took a bit of searching but eventually he spotted a cabin with the number 23 on it. He stopped well short of the cabin, parked the car, and turned off the engine. He sat in silence collecting his thoughts as he heard the ticking of the engine. He looked up at the cabin again. A light was on but he didn't see any movement. He took a deep breath and thought "here goes nothing."

He walked up to the cabin. It was well kept. It had a small porch in the front that led to the front door. He walked up the steps and then to the door. He opened the screen door and knocked. A few seconds later the door opened and he was now face to face with Beth.

She stood frozen for several minutes just gazing at him. Carl could not read her expression.

Carl shifted his weight and that seemed to snap Beth out of her trance.

"Carl? What are you doing here?" she said in disbelief.

"It's a long story. I know this is overwhelming, but may I come in?"

Beth hesitated. "Umm. Sure."

She held the door open for Carl. As he walked by, he could smell her perfume. It was the same perfume she had when they were together. His mind was going 100 miles per hour. Beth led them through the entryway and into the kitchen and dining room area. She kept a nice clean house just like Carl remembered. Carl glanced around and saw pictures of Beth and her former husband that passed away. They both sat down at the dining room table.

"Do you want something to drink?" Beth asked.

"Sure, I'd have some coffee"

Beth already had a pot of coffee ready and poured Carl a cup. She set it in front of him, filled her cup up and sat back down.

"Carl, why are you here?"

Carl glanced down at his hands and had to stop himself from shaking. He had rehearsed in his mind for 17 years how he would go about this discussion.

"As I said. It is a long story. I know you remember Kevin and Lily Johnson?"

"Of course. How could I forget?"

"They have a son named Buddy. He is a senior this year. One heck of an athlete."

"I know. Lily and I are friends on Facebook."

"Oh. Of course. I'm not really up on my social media."

"How does this long story have anything to do with Buddy?"

"Well, several weeks ago after a basketball game Buddy was out shooting free throws in the elementary school playground. You remember that court?"

"Yes. I remember."

"I was watching him from the living room window. Well, he got mad and kicked the ball and it shattered the window up in my office." Carl laughed. "I'd never seen anybody run that fast in my life."

Beth grinned. "So how did you handle that? Don't tell me you did the Carl Ross challenge?"

Carl smiled and shrugged. "Hey, what can I say it works!"

Beth rolled her eyes. "So how did that go?"

Carl's voice cracked as he said, "To be blunt, Buddy Johnson probably saved my life."

Beth raised her eyebrows. "What do you mean by that?"

Carl took a sip of his coffee. "Here is when the long story begins, but I will condense it as much as I can. I set up the three challenges for Buddy. It was difficult at first. We didn't really connect. As the weeks went by, I think I was learning more from Buddy than he was learning from me. Meeting with him gave me a purpose. We developed a great relationship. Because of him I started focusing on the Bible again. I quit drinking. I sleep more. I exercise daily. You see Beth, with you I hit rock bottom after Kevin's death. Then when you left, which was the right thing for you to do, I went deeper into depression. Beth, I had thoughts daily of taking my own life. Then, when I was to the point I didn't think I could go on anymore, God put Buddy Johnson into my life." Carl was crying at this point and had to stop to continue. "So I talked Buddy into riding out here with me to see you. I need to make it right between us."

Beth was quiet for several seconds. "Why couldn't you change sooner for me?" she said almost as a whisper.

"That is the biggest mistake I've ever made in my life and I have regretted it since the day you left. All I'm asking now is forgiveness and a second chance. I don't know what the future holds but I do know I want you to be a part of it. I just need a one word answer. Say no and I will get up right now and leave. Say yes and I promise I will be the Carl you knew back in college and our early years of marriage."

Beth looked down at her coffee. "I need time to think about this. This is a lot right now."

"I understand. Buddy and I are leaving today because he needs to get back for his summer job.

Here is my cell number when you have an answer."
Buddy slid his business card to the center of the
table. He then got up and headed towards the door.
Beth followed.

"It was really nice to see and talk to you
Beth. I look forward to hearing from you."

"Same here, Carl. Drive safe."

Carl got back into his car and took a deep
breath. She was the most beautiful person in the
world. She still gave him butterflies. He now did
what he had started doing again since meeting
Buddy. He prayed.

Buddy

Carl pulled up in front of Buddy's house. The trip back had been great. He had really developed a great relationship with Carl. Buddy got out and put his forearms on the bottom of the open window and leaned down to talk to Carl.

"When do you think she will call?" Buddy asked.

Carl put his head down. "I don't know. The Beth I know was always a thinker. She would analyze everything before making a decision. I hope soon because I think about it all the time."

"I'm sure she will call soon."

Right after the words left his mouth Carl's cell phone started ringing. Carl looked down.

"It's a Montana area code!" He just stared at
it.

"Go on. Answer it!" said Buddy.

Carl pushed the answer button. "Hello. Hi
Beth." He glanced over at Buddy with wide eyes.
He was sweating. "Ok. Yep. I see. Ok. Yep. Ok.
Thanks. Bye, Beth." Carl looked down at the phone
and pushed the end button and just stared at the
phone.

"Well, old timer…what did she say?"

Carl took a deep breath and looked up at
Buddy with tears in his eyes. Then he slowly got a
grin on his face and said, "She said yes."

Questions for Reflection

The Incident

- ❖ How do you deal with failure?

- ❖ Have failures contributed to your anger?

- ❖ How can a person use failure and anger as a source of strength?

- ❖ What does the Bible say about anger?

- ❖ Do you judge others before you get to know them?

- ❖ When Buddy entered Carl's life it brought back a bad memory from Carl's past. How can we as individuals cope with mistakes we have made?

Challenge #1

- ❖ What is your attitude when you must do something you don't want to do?

- ❖ Carl immediately made Buddy feel comforted. Have you been around individuals that are the same way? What is it about people that have that effect?

- ❖ Buddy grew up without a father. How is a father figure important for children?

- ❖ Carl talks about the word "SEE" for challenge #1. Do you "SEE" people daily?

- ❖ Does God provide you daily with the opportunity to make an influence? How do you respond to that opportunity?

- ❖ What are your thoughts on the quote "I want to be a reflection of Him?"

- ❖ Carl said when he read the Bible his way of life changed. What do you think that means?

- ❖ John 13:34 says 'a new command I give you; Love one another. As I have loved you, so you must love one another'. How can that verse relate to your daily life?

Challenge #2

❖ We have a choice daily to be positive or negative. How hard is it to make that choice?

❖ Carl talks about the word "CONNECT" for challenge #2. How do you "CONNECT" with people daily?

❖ How does Matthew 4:18 relate to the word connect?

❖ When Buddy tried to connect with Jacob, he struggled to make a connection. How have you handled a similar situation?

❖ How was Buddy able to connect with Jacob?

Challenge #3

❖ How can following Jesus help you be the light in the lives of others?

❖ Carl talks about the word "LEAD" for challenge #3. How do you "LEAD" people daily?

❖ What does it mean to be a "Servant Leader?"

❖ John Wooden is one example Buddy uses as a great leader. What other leaders do you like to look to for guidance?

❖ In John 13:1-20, Jesus washes his disciples' feet. How is this leadership?

❖ How can living out the "Servant Leadership Cycle" create a life of significance?

The Trip

- ❖ Have you ever decided to take a risk? What thoughts go through your mind?

- ❖ How did Buddy and Carl thrive off each other to create a lasting relationship? How did Buddy "save" Carl's life?

- ❖ Does Carl deserve forgiveness? What does the Bible say about forgiveness?

- ❖ How can the story relate to Faith, Forgiveness, and Friendship?